To a girl who is at the very top of her league, wether it be golf or being the best buddy ever.

X

HUMOURS OF GOLF

HUMOURS OF GOLF

BY
W. HEATH ROBINSON

with an introduction by
BERNARD DARWIN

DUCKWORTH

Reissued 1999

Gerald Duckworth & Co. Ltd.
61 Frith Street, London W1V 5TA
Tel: 0171 434 4242
Fax: 0171 434 4420
Email: enquiries@duckworth-publishers.co.uk

First published in 1923
This edition © 1975 by The Estate of W. Heath Robinson
Foreword © 1999 by Peter Alliss

A catalogue record for this book is available
from the British Library

ISBN 0 7156 0915 7

Printed and bound in Great Britain by
Redwood Books Ltd, Trowbridge

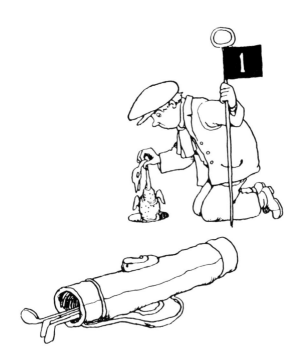

CONTENTS

FOREWORD

Peter Alliss

GOLF IS ONE of the few games that generates great slices of humour. Of course there are humorous tales of rugby, soccer, cricket and boxing, but for the life of me I don't think I've ever heard a tennis joke.

I suppose it's the cross-section of people interested in the game that makes it special. It's a pedestrian game, it doesn't have the violence of a shared ball game, although the mental side can be very significant and stressful. It's amazing when you think that nothing your opponent does can in any way interfere with the result of your shot. Oh there can be innuendo, suggestion, murmurings and moments of gamesmanship, but it's not the same as a goalkeeper making a blinding save or a slip fielder snapping up the catch of the century. I know there are people who don't understand the game, let alone play it, who pooh pooh the idea that they should ever take up golf, or they might when they're past playing rugby, cricket, soccer and other "violent" games. Golf has everything, humour, sadness, sporting courage, mistakes, silliness, even a bit of cheating, but I think that's more to do with ignorance than out-and-out villainy. Another remarkable thing about the game? – you can call a person anything but "A cheat at golf".

March 1999

INTRODUCTION

by Bernard Darwin (1923)

T O STUDY Mr. Heath Robinson's entertaining pictures is to realize how far more subtle and complex golfing humour has become since the days when the great golf "boom" first brought the golf joke with it. Those who played in the 'eighties or even the early 'nineties still remember with some little bitterness the type of joke to which their strange game gave rise. The mere word "niblick" was then exquisitely absurd: unadorned it was enough to make any reasonable man split his sides. Of pictorial jests there were two, or at most three. First there was the irascible gentleman represented breaking his clubs; next there were two companion pictures: the first, entitled "Fore," showed a golfer driving; in the second, "Aft," a stout pedestrian received the ball on some more yielding portion of his person. Now this is in a sense a primitive and eternal joke. It is like that of an old lady on a frosty day sitting down on a slide on the pavement. If we see it in real life we cannot help giggling, but we soon grow weary of it in a picture. Yet it persisted for years, perhaps because the artist could not trust his public to understand anything more recondite about the game. In this book there is, indeed, one amiable old gentleman who, having broken all his clubs, has tied the head of one of them to his wife's umbrella, but he has not broken his clubs in fury: he has only found the lies on a stony hillside something too much for him. As to the player in front who is hit behind, there is no trace of him at all.

It is, to be sure, hardly right to generalize on golfing jokes from Mr. Heath Robinson's pictures, because, whatever his subject, he is never primitive or obvious. His prodigal imagination always soars into more complicated regions. We must look at each of his drawings for some little while before we can take in all his ingenuities. Only a reader with a most comprehensive eye could get all his chuckling done at once. Sometimes he leaves us half wondering whether we have discovered everything that was in his mind. There is, for example, that picture of the two engaging lions walking away happy and replete, while on the green in the foreground is all that remains of their lunch. There is but one cap, one pipe, one club-bag. Why is that? Does Mr. Heath Robinson mean us to infer that the golfer who is so uncompanionable as to play by himself deserves to be eaten? If he ever plays on one well-known London course, where every morning a string of old gentlemen follow each other round in file at a the rate of one mile an hour, I can well believe that this was his meaning.

When first we look at the pictures in this book we may think that the golfers whom the artist has created are wholly divorced from reality, but this is not so. Golfers possess imaginations almost as fantastic as his, and some of his flights have in fact been anticipated almost by real live players. Take, for instance, the agreeable drawing of a fat man who looks rather like a Macedonian bandit armed to the teeth. Slung around his waist are various club-heads, and he fits now one and now another to his single shaft according to the exigencies of the game. Years ago there was a golfer who invented one universal club, the heads being affixed, and the degree of loft on their faces varied upon some ingenious screwing principle. The putter on rollers has long since come under the ban of the Rules of Golf Committee, and there is one, I think, to be seen in the Chamber of Horrors at St. Andrews, where are preserved those freakish children of the golfer's perverted fancy that were strangled at birth. As to the machine called the "Golf Guider for Hitting the ball on the Exact Spot," I cannot assert that this has ever been made, but one of the most famous of professionals told me that he had often thought of building a kind of spiral groove for guiding the beginner's club-head in the way it should go. Even Mr. Heath Robinson's movable bunker exists. At a certain sanatorium in Scotland, where the patients are allowed only a little gentle putting, hurdles on wheels form the hazard, and the course is altered week by week.

The jokes about golfers who indulge in paroxysms of rage are now rather antiquated. Golfers have today grown so much better tempered, or at least so much less demonstrative than of old, that they accept their mishaps almost with the impassivity of the professional billiard player. Gone long since is the player who threw all his clubs into the sea, and then, in a fit of remorse, nearly drowned himself in the retrieving of them. Once he had many fellows, but he has them no longer. Gone, too, is that kindliest and most delightful of golfers who once solemnly called down fire and brimstone on a Prestwick putting green, who would administer corporal chastisement to his clubs when they misbehaved, battering his stumpy little putter against the wall with the words, "You little devil, don't you presume on my good nature any longer!" Where is he who, not content with throwing his bag of clubs into a pond, went back to the clubhouse, disinterred his reserves from his locker, and made a bonfire of them, feeding the flames, when they showed signs of dying down, with his old boots.

And yet, thank goodness, they are not all quite gone, these heroic jokers. One of the best tempered of my golfing acquaintances once, in cold, deliberate anger, drove several miles to a railway line and watched his clubs being reduced to spillikins by a passing express. I hope soon again to be playing with another friend who threw his driver so far and so deep into the whins that he had to say to the couple behind, "Will you please come on, sir. I've lost my club."

I always chuckle when I think of him, not without a shamefaced sensation of throwing stones in a glass-house, for I am conscious that my own clubs might sometimes have been lost had there been a gorse-bush handy. I cannot help chuckling largely because I know that particular golfer, and that is the worst of most golfing jokes. There is so strong a personal element in them. They depend, to some extent at any rate, on our knowing the people. My mind misgives me that, when some day that collection of the Scottish professional's sayings is handed secretly round to a later generation, they will not appreciate them, because they never knew the incomparable air and vigour with which they were delivered. They may even say that their elders were stupid fellows who were very easily amused.

To drawbacks of this kind Mr. Heath Robinson's humour is not subject. His golfers do not belong to any particular time or course. True, when I contemplate the drawing of the gentleman about to putt being startled by a small fish leaping out of the hole, I am reminded that in a peculiarly wet winter fish were caught on the fourth green of a London course. At least a member of the club assured me that this was so, and I would name the course but that I fear the committee would "have the law on me." In any case, that is but a small point. Mr. Heath Robinson's golfers are not often likely to be identified with those who play on any course now known to us. They are in their essence impersonal and perennial, and we should be grateful to him accordingly. One or two of his pictures may possibly grow out of date; that of the "stymie bridge," for instance, wherein the player lofts his ball into a neat little tunnel, held by his caddie, which will conduct it straight into the hole over the intervening obstacle. There are today some people who are anxious to abolish what they call the "unfairness" of golf. If they ever come into power there will be no stymies, and the golfer of the future, gazing at that picture, will refuse to believe that anything so monstrous was ever permitted as that one player's ball should get in the way of the other's. That golfer of the future will not understand Mr. Heath Robinson's joke, but by that time golf will be such a huge joke in itself that it will not matter.

BERNARD DARWIN

THE FALL OF MAN

(1)

A Wet Season

HOW COAL WAS FIRST DISCOVERED IN SCOTLAND

(3)

*Styles in **Stance**—I*

SOME FOURSOME

For the Weary Caddy

AN INTELLIGENT GREEN-KEEPER AT 2.0 A.M., DISGUISED AS AN EARLY BIRD, SCARING WORMS FROM A GOLFING GREEN

SOME CURIOUS CASES OF LOST BALL

(8)

WHEN SPRING HANDICAPS

Pyramid Golf

SOME NEW WATER SPORTS FOR THE SEASIDE HOLIDAYS

IMPROVED GOLF CLUBS

MORE IMPROVED GOLF

The Bent Niblick for Curly Bunker Work

THE FORLORN HOPE

(15)

An Awkward Lie

POGO GOLF FOR 18-HOLE COURSES

Half Time

FORE !

THE GREEN

AQUATIC GOLF—I

A COMMON MISTAKE

BUNKERED

W. HEATH ROBINSON

AQUATIC GOLF—II

THE LOST BALL.

AQUATIC GOLF—III

(21)

THE TEE

HEATH ROBINSON

AQUATIC GOLF—IV

(22)

REMARKABLE AVUNCULAR COINCIDENCE AT ONE OF THE NEW GOLF COURSES IN PALESTINE

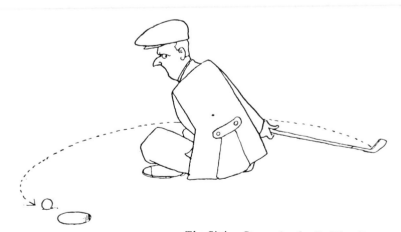

The Sitting Stance for the Budding Putter

HOW NOAH MANAGED TO KEEP HIS HAND IN DURING THE FLOOD

SPRING CLEANING OF GOLF COURSE IN READINESS FOR THE SPRING SEASON

HOLED!

SHOWING THE UNFORTUNATE EFFECT OF NOT KEEPING YOUR EYE ON THE BALL

Another Awkward Lie

THE RECORD

Patent Putter with adjustment for levelling out worm casts

THE ST. ANDREW'S BUNKER CHAIR, DESIGNED TO RELIEVE GOLFERS OF THE NECESSITY OF
WALKING ROUND BUNKERS

(31)

W. HEATH ROBINSON.

GOLF BRACES -
FOR FACILE MOVEMENTS

THE NEW OUTFIT—FOR
DISPENSING WITH CADDIES

THE NEW
PUTTING TROWSERS - FOR
BENDING OVER THE GREEN

THE HILL-SIDE CLUTCH

SOME GOLFING NOVELTIES FOR THE NEXT SEASON—I

SOME GOLFING NOVELTIES FOR THE NEXT SEASON—II

The new adjustable Tee

THE NEW GOLF CAR FOR THE COMFORT OF GOLFERS

THE ORIGIN OF PLUS FOURS

RISKS AND LIABILITIES COVERED BY THE NEW " HEATH ROBINSON " INSURANCE SCHEME FOR GOLFERS

ONE IN TWO
A TRAGEDY OF THE SAHARA GOLF COURSE

(39)

Style in Stance—II

Style in Stance—III

THE LAST HOLE BEFORE THE FLOOD

SOME SUGGESTIONS FOR THE GOLFING NOVICE

SOME INTERESTING METHODS OF PROPAGANDA TO SECURE THE GOLFING VOTE

To vary the Monotony of the Game

A NEW ADJUSTMENT FOR GOLF BALLS WHICH SUCCESSFULLY DISCLOSES THEIR WHEREABOUTS

The Caddy's Friend

TOO MUCH VIM

(47)

Après Vous

THE ANNUAL GET-THERE-FIRST GOLFING HANDICAP, WHICH SHOULD BE A FEATURE OF
ALL FUTURE GOLF FESTIVALS

The End